SUSTAINING OUR ENVIRONMENT
Cities

Jill Laidlaw

W
FRANKLIN WATTS
LONDON • SYDNEY

First published in 2009 by
Franklin Watts
338 Euston Road
London NW1 3BH

Franklin Watts Australia
Level 17/207 Kent Street
Sydney NSW 2000

Series editor: Adrian Cole
Art director: Jonathan Hair
Design: Simon Borrough
Picture research: Diana Morris

Acknowledgements:
Aguilarphoto/Shutterstock: 40. Arco Images/Alamy: 28. John Arnold/Alamy: 32. Tom Bonaventure/Getty Images: 12. Celsopupo/istockphoto: 11c. China Photos/Getty Images: 19t. Edgedigital/istockphoto: 26. Daniel Garcia/AFP/Getty Images: 11t. greeningofdetroit.com: 19b. © dbox for Cook+Fox Architects: 20. Green Roofs for Healthy Cities/greenroofs.org: 21. Jason Hawkes/Getty Images: 15. Mark Henley/Panos: 13, 25. Kamal Jufri/Panos: 36. Cezaro de Luca/epa/Corbis: 34. Carsten Madsen/istockphoto: 30. David McNew/Getty Images: 37. Tony Morrison/South American Pictures: 16. Nikada/Istockphoto: 38. Norcal Waste Systems Inc: 33. Olly/Shutterstock: front cover. George Osodi/Panos: 35. Mikkel Ostergaard/Panos: 10. Martin Roemers/Panos: 29t. Steve Rossef/istockphoto: 14. Licia Rubenstein/istockphoto: 24. Karim Sahib/AFP/Getty Images: 29b. Issouf Sanogo/AFP/Getty Images: 8. Alex Segre/PD: 27. SF New Developments. All Rights Reserved: 23. Jacob Silberberg/Panos: 18, 22. Paul Smith/Panos: 17b. Steve Speller/PD: 41. Tomograf/istockphoto: 31. Lee Torrens/istockphoto: 17t. Peter Usbeck/Alamy: 39. Webphotographer/istockphoto: 9.

Every attempt has been made to clear copyright. Should there be any inadvertent omission please apply to the publisher for rectification.

A CIP catalogue record for this book is available from the British Library.

Dewey number: 307.76

ISBN: 978 0 7496 8828 8

Printed in China

Franklin Watts is a division of Hachette Children's Books, an Hachette UK company.
www.hachette.co.uk

Contents

Sustainable cities

Over time, human beings have changed from living in mostly rural areas to mostly urban environments. In 2008, for the first time, the majority of people in the world lived in cities. This movement of people from the countryside to the city looks set to continue. It is predicted that 70 per cent of the world's population will live in cities by 2050.

City statistics
- In Australia 90 per cent of people live in cities.
- In the USA 81 per cent of people live in cities.
- In Europe 72 per cent of people live in cities.
- In China 40 per cent of people live in cities.
- In India 29 per cent of people live in cities.
- One million people worldwide move to a city to live every week.
- In 1900, only 16 cities in the world had a population of over 1 million – now 400 cities do.

▲ A man selling shirts in Yaounde, Cameroon's capital city. Global goods and services industries are providing more work than agriculture. This has brought about a rapid growth of city populations as people have moved into urban areas to find jobs.

The best and worst of cities

Why are millions of people moving to cities? Because cities can be places of fantastic possibilities – where access to education and employment can be fairer and more abundant, and life expectancy longer and infant mortality lower.

However, cities can mean misery for millions of people. Within cities there are great divides between the rich and the poor, and many people have to endure restricted access to utilities, such as water and electricity, little or unaffordable public transport, bad housing, inadequate sanitation and poor schools or healthcare facilities.

Environmental impacts

Cities have many negative environmental impacts, one of which is the production of huge amounts of carbon dioxide (CO_2), a greenhouse gas that is thought to be one of the central causes of man-made global warming. But the density of people located in cities offers us real opportunities to re-order and control the way we live, ushering in energy efficiency on a huge scale, enforcing environmental laws, and implementing waste reduction schemes and good public transport.

What is a sustainable city?

A sustainable city has the ability to exist without causing lasting damage to the environment. This depends on the impact of all the things the city consumes, including water, electricity and food. It also depends on all of the things a city creates, such as manufactured goods and pollution. Things that add to people's quality of life also need to be considered, such as good air quality and access to green space, as do things that damage quality of life, such as the mismanagement of waste disposal. To be sustainable in the long term, cities must have systems to monitor and control these factors, and to provide public services to people at all levels of society.

'A sustainable city is a city where achievements in social, economic, and physical development are made to last.'

From The Sustainable Cities Programme (SCP) (a joint facility of the United Nations Centre for Human Settlements (Habitat) and the United Nations Environment Programme (UNEP), 1990s

▼ **Looking across Boat Quay and the Central Business District in Singapore. Many people are attracted to cities because they can be exciting places to live.**

What do cities need?

A city can be thought of as a great big machine that consumes certain things – such as oxygen, water, timber, plastics, paper, cement, glass and metals – to keep functioning, expanding and developing. These great 'beasts of consumption' also excrete a lot of things, including industrial sludge, digested food pumped out of the city as sewage and discarded consumer goods.

Case study...
Denmark: the city of Kalundborg

Kalundborg is a city that has become 'circular' in the way that it functions. Over the past 40 years, businesses have reorganised the way they work so that they have become mutually beneficial (see below). This means that Kalundborg now has more in common with a natural ecosystem than most conventional cities.

- The refinery supplies excess gas to the plasterboard factory.
- The local coal-powered power station (above) supplies 'waste' steam to heat residents' houses and water – this system replaced about 3,500 domestic oil furnaces and so improved air quality in the city. (All the steam from most power stations is discharged into the atmosphere.)
- Waste sludge from the biotech factory and the fish farm's water treatment plant is used on nearby farmland.
- The power station uses salt water from the nearby fjord for cooling, which saves freshwater for drinking. The hot salt water byproduct is sold to local fish farms so they can manage salt-water levels in their tanks.

> 'Blaming cities for greenhouse gas emissions misses the point that cities are a large part of the solution . . . Well planned, well governed cities can provide high living standards that do not require high consumption levels and high greenhouse gas emissions.'
>
> David Satterthwaite, Senior Fellow at the International Institute for Environment and Development (IIED), 2008

▲ The Earth Summit in Rio in 1992 was an important step in raising the consciousness of governments around the world about sustainable development issues.

Feeding the city

In the natural world, every part of an ecosystem is dependent on another aspect of the same environment. For example, one animal's waste can fertilise land that grows a plant that is another animal's food. This cycle of life is mutually beneficial to everything in its environment – it is balanced. But many cities are not in balance with their surroundings, taking what they need. This includes clean water for drinking, cooking and washing; and fossil fuels for private and public transport, and to power electricity production for heating or cooling properties, lighting streets and homes. These cities don't operate in a 'circular' way like

the natural environment. They function in a non-circular or linear way that is unsustainable, causing destruction and waste.

Turning points – Rio and Aalborg

In 1992, the United Nations Conference on Environment and Development (UNCED), known as the Earth Summit, took place in Rio de Janeiro, Brazil. At the conference, representatives from 178 countries discussed many aspects of the environment. One of the most important themes was sustainability – particularly how

◀ The beachfront of Rio de Janeiro, Brazil. Cities occupy only 2 per cent of the world's land area but consume between 40 per cent and 75 per cent of the world's resources.

to improve urban sustainability. One of the outcomes of the meeting was the establishment of Agenda 21, an 800-page global action plan for sustainable development. Agenda 21 recognised the importance of tackling urban environmental issues and it has since been implemented around the world – with varying degrees of success.

In 1994, the Aalborg Charter (named after the town in Denmark where it was created and signed) paved the way for the European Sustainable Cities and Towns Campaign. European cities and towns that sign up to the Charter commit to developing their urban environments in a sustainable way.

Cities worlds apart

The thing that cities all over the world have in common is the aspirations of the people who live there. These aspirations are the same no matter what the race, culture or language of the city's inhabitants – everyone wants to work towards a better life. So cities all over the world have a great deal in common. However, cities are also different – geography, history, climate conditions and population shifts mean that they take unique shapes and have unique problems as well.

'Cities embody some of society's most pressing challenges, from pollution and disease to unemployment and lack of adequate shelter. But cities are also venues where rapid, dramatic change is not just possible but expected.'

Ban Ki-moon, Secretary-General, United Nations, from the Foreword of the UN HABITAT State of the World's Cities Report, 2008/09

◀ Mexico City's population has grown rapidly in recent years. An estimated 4 million people live here in Neza-Chalco-Itza, Mexico City, making it the largest slum in the world.

Cities in less developed countries

The main areas of urban growth are currently in less developed countries (LDCs). Around 90 per cent of the world's new cities of over 1 million people have appeared in Asia in the last decade. Managing this expansion is the greatest problem they face. For example, 400,000 people move to Delhi, India, from rural areas every year in search of work. Most of these people are economic migrants: people looking for a better life. With two-thirds of the rural population in LDCs living below the poverty line (in cities this figure is about a third), people regard cities as being better places to live.

Cities in more developed countries

People in cities in more developed countries (MDCs) demand high standards of public transport, energy provision, education, healthcare, entertainment and food. These expectations have a negative impact on natural resources, such as water and fossil fuels. While some new cities are appearing in MDCs and existing ones are expanding, other cities are in decline and facing problems, such as run-down housing and city centres that are in need of renewal.

◀ Tokyo, Japan, as it is today. But in the 1970s, clouds of sulphur dioxide covered the city. People suffered from eye infections and respiratory diseases.

Case study…
Air pollution in Tokyo and Mexico City

Many cities have taken significant steps to deal with environmental problems, but how effective these are often depends on the resources available and the stage of urban development.

Cities in MDCs are usually wealthy and at a more advanced stage of development. For example, in the early 1970s, the air in Toyko, Japan, was highly polluted. Action had to be taken to clean it up. Over the following decades, the government passed new laws to restrict the types of petrol that vehicles could use, and clamped down on emissions from factories. Today, Tokyo's air is much healthier.

Cities in LDCs are often poorer and at an earlier stage of development. For example, in 1992, the United Nations found the air in Mexico City, Mexico, to be the most polluted in the world. Over the last ten years, the Mexican government has enforced the use of unleaded petrol and there are compulsory 'No Driving Days'. However, Mexico City still has a very long way to go before its air is clean.

The domination of cities

The relationship between cities and the areas that surround them is closely intertwined and of vital importance – cities need the countryside and the countryside needs cities.

Cities need the towns, villages and farms that surround them to supply an additional labour force and natural resources, such as energy (from power stations located beyond city boundaries) and food (grown in nearby productive land), as well as leisure opportunities. Cities provide rural communities with employment, leisure, entertainment and educational opportunities and a market for their goods.

> 'The two-word definition of sustainability is "one planet".'
> Mathis Wackernagel, Swiss-born ecologist

Cities and the world

Cities consume such vast amounts of resources that they cannot be supplied by the surrounding areas alone. Cities buy and sell goods and services on a global scale in order to support their populations, and so their economic links with other parts of the world are often just as strong as their economic ties to their home nation.

Ecological footprint

The influence of cities reaches beyond the suburbs or shanty towns that mark the edges of a metropolis. In the 1990s, the ecologists Mathis Wackernagel and William Rees came up with the concept of the 'ecological footprint'. This means the amount of land a person, city or country needs to support their lives or population, for example the food eaten, the clothes worn, the water consumed and the rubbish thrown away.

◀ **The city of Vancouver, Canada, has an ecological footprint 200 times its own size.**

'We do not have an ecological crisis. The ecosphere has a human crisis. Our "story" about our place in the scheme of things has somehow gone awry in the industrial age…'

William Rees, Canadian ecologist

▼ London is the most dominant city in Britain, with a population of around 7.5 million people.

Footprint facts

If we look at ecological footprints, the inequalities between peoples become obvious:

• There is 1.5 hectares of productive land available for every person on Earth.
• The 1.1-billion-strong population of India uses an average of 0.4 of a hectare of productive land per person; this is around half a tennis court each.
• Americans use an average of 11.75 hectares of land each – about the size of ten football pitches each.
• If everyone in the world becomes as rich as Americans we will need three planets to live on.
• Britain has an ecological footprint eight times its size.

Case study…
Britain: London's ecological footprint

Only 12 per cent of Britain's population lives in London, but it has been calculated that London needs an area of productive land 120 times the size of the city itself to meet its needs. So although London only takes up about 1,500 square kilometres, it needs about 20 million square kilometres of land to supply it with the things it needs, such as energy, food and waste facilities. If London were forced to use only land in the UK to meet its needs, the city would use up all the productive land in Britain. However, in reality, London uses the resources of the world to fuel itself, including steel from India, wheat from the USA, rice from Asia, consumer goods from Japan, timber from Scandinavia, fuel from Russia and meat from Europe.

Nature in the city

Cities – the houses, streets, roads, factories and offices – literally pave over green space where animals and plants could thrive. Wherever it takes place, bad urban planning – or a lack of urban planning – ignores green space in the race to maximise financial returns on residential and office developments, leaving people and the planet shortchanged.

Urban sprawl

In Europe, greenbelt areas – protected areas of land around the edges of cities – were established from the late 1940s onwards to prevent cities creeping into the countryside. Many countries recognised that their cities were growing to accommodate workers in low-rise, single unit homes in newly expanding suburbs. Cities began to encroach on rural land and this became known as 'urban sprawl'. Today urban sprawl includes out-of-town retail parks, office space and thousands of kilometres of new roads – further extending the influence, and pollution, of cities.

Case study...
Brazil: Curitiba

The city of Curitiba (below) in Brazil is home to 1.8 million people and is known as the ecological capital of Brazil. Since the 1960s, Curitiba has implemented innovative urban plans to improve the quality of life for its inhabitants and to preserve biodiversity. Curitiba has incorporated 28 parks, 14 forests and more than 1,000 green spaces into its residential areas so that 20 per cent of the city is now green space. More than 1.5 million trees have been planted in residential areas since the 1970s. Tax breaks are given to builders who make sure that green space is incorporated into their developments, and street children are supported by planting and maintaining flower gardens on land reclaimed from derelict buildings and wasteland.

▲ Part of the bus network in Curitiba, Brazil. Having an efficient public transport network in the city reduces the space needed for more roads and car parks.

'The cities will determine the fate of the remaining biodiversity of our planet . . . the battle for life will be won or lost there.'

Ahmed Djoghlaf, Executive Secretary of the UN Convention on Biological Diversity, 2007

Greening the city

Green space in cities can be maximised by creating and protecting parks, city farms and wildlife gardens. Many cities are making efforts to create wildlife corridors by replanting disused urban space such as old railway tracks. These nature thoroughfares improve air quality and bring down the temperature of city centres in hot weather to reduce the amount of energy needed to keep homes cool. Any urban space that isn't covered in concrete – grass verges alongside pavements, traffic islands and roundabouts – can be turned into a haven for plants and animals.

▲ Urban parks, such as this one in Melbourne, Australia, can help to bring wildlife back into cities.

Green space facts

• In Tokyo 5 per cent of land is given over to green space.
• In Los Angeles 10 per cent of the city is green space.
• In London 46 per cent of the city is green space.

Food grown in cities

One of the ways green space is being brought back into cities is through allotments and city farms. City farms used to be very common – a century ago Paris supplied itself with fruit and vegetables by using a sixth of its land area for farming, fertilised by horse manure. But, with the arrival of cars and trains, food could be transported from the countryside, leading to the start of 'food miles' (the distance food is transported from production to plate). Now cities import food from all over the world – fish from Scottish lochs is flown to restaurants in Barcelona within hours of being caught.

▲ A city farmer tends to his plants on a roof-top garden in Pudong District, Shanghai, China.

Case study... China: Shanghai

Shanghai uses the tonnes of human waste produced every day to fertilise city farm plots and the land that surrounds the city (called peri-urban land). These urban farm spaces provide about 90 per cent of the city's milk and eggs, 60 per cent of its vegetables, and 50 per cent of the pork and poultry needed.

'Through urban agriculture, we hope to increase the poor's self-confidence, and so increase their participation in society.'

Leonardo Gil Mora, Vice Minister of Integrated Rural Development, Caracas, Venezuela, 2006

Awareness of urban farming

A tradition of urban cultivation is still very much alive today in many cities around the world. In Europe and America there are huge waiting lists for gardeners wishing to grow vegetables on allotments, or plots of community land and the rise of farmer's markets (markets selling locally sourced produce) is an indicator of the awareness that city-dwellers now have of the unsustainable aspects of food miles.

Urban farming lifelines

Urban farming is vital to the food security of cities in politically unstable nations and in cities with a large proportion of people living below the poverty line. In many LDCs, urban farming is a part of the normal functioning of the city.

• In Hanoi, Vietnam, 80 per cent of the vegetables and 50 per cent of the pork and poultry eaten in the city are farmed in the city or on the land right next to the city.

• Rooftop gardens in Dakar, Senegal, yield 30 kg of tomatoes per square metre every year.

• Four thousand microgardens – each only one square metre in size – in Caracas, Venezuela, provide the poorest inhabitants of the city with 330 lettuces and up to 16 kg of cabbage each every year.

▼ **Tending vegetable crops in a government-run city garden, Caracas, Venezuela. The Venezuelan government hopes to produce the majority of the city's food in this way.**

Campaign··· USA: Greening of Detroit

The Greening of Detroit is a campaign to utilise the city's derelict land. The campaign trains people in urban farming, tests soil, provides compost, seeds and plants, and helps to turn wasteland into productive land that gives residents a steady supply of fruit and vegetables. Greening of Detroit's Garden Resource Program has transformed over 200 community plots – which now produce just over 100 tonnes of food every year.

▶ **Children learn about plants on one of the Greening Detroit projects. Over a three-year period Greening Detroit created Romanowski Park, an urban farm covering 10.5 hectares within the city.**

Green building

Cities are declining and expanding at such a rapid rate that they are in a permanent state of change. From hotels to schools, structures are being built right now, many times over, all over the world.

Sustainable construction

Most new public buildings are like plastic food containers, sealed on all sides with windows that cannot open, artificially cooled in summer, and expensively-heated in the winter. Structures of this type cost a lot to construct in the first place – they use huge amounts of natural resources such as water, steel and fossil fuels – and they also cost a lot to maintain. Some scientists think that buildings account for over 50 per cent of worldwide carbon dioxide emissions. If we try to control and reinvent methods of construction, and we rethink the aims of architecture, then we can move forward with sustainability.

'Architects have a vital role as advocates of sustainable solutions.'

Norman Foster, architect, 2005

Case study···
USA: Bank of America Tower, One Bryant Park, New York City

The Bank of America Tower, one of the world's most environmentally sensitive large-scale construction projects, was completed in 2008 on the island of Manhattan in New York. The Tower was mostly constructed out of recycled and recyclable materials and all new materials were sourced within 800 kilometres of the site. The building has a grey-water system that collects rainwater and wastewater and re-uses it, as well as carbon dioxide monitors that maintain fresh air at the correct level. A combined heat and power (CHP) plant has been built on site to supply the Tower with a power source and useful heat.

▶ The Bank of America Tower has been given a platinum LEED award – the highest environmental certification in the USA (see opposite page).

'The new Tower – which will stand as one of the world's most environmentally responsible high-rise buildings – is a shining example of how you can create jobs while also protecting the environment.'

George Pataki, Governor of New York, talking about the Bank of America Tower, 2004

Campaign... England: brownfield sites

Through its Housing Sprawl Campaign, the Campaign to Protect Rural England (CPRE) puts pressure on local councils to identify and use brownfield sites (areas within cities that have become derelict, such as car parks) rather than building on previously undeveloped land. This campaign pressure has had an effect – in England in 1997, 56 per cent of all new houses were built on brownfield land, but by 2007, 77 per cent of all new homes built in England were built on brownfield sites.

Green standards

Some governments are putting environmental building codes into practice – but many remain voluntary. In the USA, LEED (Leadership in Energy and Environmental Design) is a green building rating system that takes the sustainability of the building site into account. It looks at water and energy efficiency, demands minimum standards for the interior environmental quality of a building, and examines the construction materials and resources. Similar schemes are run in Australia (called Green Star) and the UK (called BREEAM: Building Research Establishment Environmental Assessment Method). All these green codes can be applied to new and existing buildings. Making old buildings environmentally sustainable is called 'retrofitting'.

'Rating tools like BREEAM, LEED and Green Star have a proven track record in driving significant improvements in performance, and I'm delighted they are now coming together to help create an international language that will enable us to talk with one voice about the vital role green buildings can play in creating a low-carbon future.'

Paul King, Chief Executive of the UK Green Building Council, 2009

▶ This is the Ballard Library in Seattle, Washington. It was built using selected recycled materials and has a roof of grass and sedum. Roof-mounted solar panels generate electricity.

Planned housing

There are many different types of planned housing in cities – from high-rise luxury apartments, exclusive private gated communities, and detached homes with gardens and garages in the suburbs, to overcrowded tower blocks.

'We shape our buildings, and afterwards our buildings shape us.'

Winston Churchill, speech, 1943

Sustainable housing

The most sustainable type of housing is multi-storey, also known as high-density, where hundreds or even thousands of people live on a relatively small piece of land. If there are local amenities, such as banks and shops, cinemas and doctors' surgeries, within walking distance, these communities become even more sustainable because the need for cars is lessened and so energy consumption and pollution are significantly reduced.

▲ The city of Hong Kong manages to cram 1,700 people on to every hectare in the district of Kowloon. A hectare is roughly the size of two football pitches.

Case study... Hong Kong: homes in the sky

Some cities have such a restricted land area that they have no choice but to build upwards. In places like Singapore and Hong Kong most people live in high-rise blocks of flats. Residential towers in Hong Kong routinely rise up for 50 storeys and are clustered together in so-called 'Harmony' blocks with their own shops, banks, hawker centres (food stalls and restaurants), schools, car parks, communal gardens and bus services. People live very closely to one another: an estate of about 20 Harmony blocks is home to 25,000–30,000 people, which is about the same number of people in a provincial town – but crammed into an area the size of a large school with its own sports grounds.

'The Eastern Neighborhoods Plans propose to provide "complete neighborhoods", including open space, improved public transit, streetscape improvements, community facilities and affordable housing.'

San Francisco Planning Department, USA, 2008

Changing behaviour

For some people, high-density housing is associated with low social status and a poor quality of life. But as old low-density buildings are demolished, governments need to find ways to persuade people to live in the homes that replace them – and these homes need to be high-density in order to be sustainable. Some cities are offering to build more community resources for people who agree to move into higher-density housing. Others, such as San Francisco in its Eastern Neighborhoods Plans (see below), make contractors pay towards local amenities as they redevelop and rezone areas for greater densities of people.

Urban planning

Urban planners can make a big difference in the move towards sustainable cities. When redeveloping areas of cities, urban planners take the following kinds of things into account:

• Efficient land use.
• Improving the ratio of green space to urban space.
• Good transport links.
• The preservation of local identities.
• Well-designed, energy-efficient housing.

▼ **Map showing the development of Eastern San Francisco. Part of the planning process included rezoning areas from industrial to residential.**

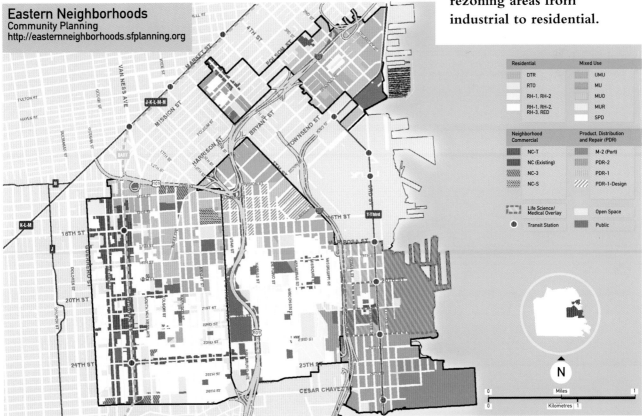

Eastern Neighborhoods
Community Planning
http://easternneighborhoods.sfplanning.org

Unplanned housing

As much as a third of the world's urban population are thought to be living in slums. Some slums have grown up over decades and some, such as Dharavi in Mumbai (see case study), have been established for over a century.

'I strongly believe that the West has much to learn from societies and places which, while sometimes poorer in material terms, are infinitely richer in the ways in which they live and organise themselves as communities. It may be the case that in a few years' time such communities will be perceived as best equipped to face the challenges that confront us because they have a built-in resilience and genuinely durable ways of living.'

Prince Charles, Foundation for the Built Environment, 2009

▼ Some slums that were once on the outskirts of cities now occupy valuable land within cities thanks to rapid urban expansion. As developing cities clear slums to build office blocks and luxury apartments (below), slum dwellers find that they have few rights because they do not own the land they live on.

Case study...
India: Life in a slum

Dharavi is the name of the slum in Mumbai, India, where the film *Slumdog Millionaire* was filmed. Dharavi is only three square kilometres in size but it is home to between 600,000 and 1 million people – no one knows for sure. Dharavi has more than 80 neighbourhoods and every one of them is a hive of activity, with clothing sweatshops, pottery workshops and leather tanning businesses. Recycling takes place everywhere because all rubbish is reused. For example, children collect plastic toys off rubbish heaps and then take them to grinding machines in the slum which chop them up and re-mould them into fake Barbie dolls.

▼ Developers want to clear Dharavi slum and build 23-storey apartment blocks there instead. The residents of Dharavi are fighting the plans.

'Many developing countries look to the West as a model but that cannot be the model. These [western] buildings use too much power and would not be affordable for us.'

Jockin Arputham, founder of the National Slum Dwellers Federation in India and resident of Dharavi slum, 2009

Debate···
Lessons from slums?

Slums are sustainable communities – they build homes out of local and readily available materials, they are not wasteful of resources, they make efficient use of space, they contain a good mix of housing and businesses, and people tend to know everyone around them.

Informal settlements

The inhabitants of many slums are now becoming organised into residents associations and dislike the term 'slum', preferring instead to be called informal settlement dwellers. Slums are highly overcrowded living spaces and are rife with poverty and disease, but slum communities also set up businesses and look after themselves – many are proud of what they have achieved and are campaigning to defend the areas they live in against government bulldozers and land grabs by commercial developers. Some slum residents have set up schools, built places of worship and installed water taps, but most slums around the world continue to provide only the most basic shelter and offer no security, amenities or hope.

With the urban population of the world set to rise from 50 per cent to 70 per cent by 2050 (with most of this expansion taking place in the developing world) can we afford to ignore the way slum communities operate? Should we be learning lessons from them rather than forcing them to accept developed-world housing solutions? Have developed-world housing solutions got it right?

Transport

The most sustainable way to travel is on foot or by bicycle, but the distance that can be travelled is limited. In many cities cars are the most common method of transport. An average city consumes 26 per cent of its total energy usage via transport, and privately-owned cars are responsible for most of this figure.

Tackling cars

With the spread of suburbs and under-investment in public transport systems, cars – and the pollution they produce – have become a large part of city life. Many people need cars to get to work or to go shopping or visit leisure centres. Various policies can be put in place to try to stop people using their cars as much as they do:

• car-pooling encourages people to share cars – every car shared to full capacity takes between four and six others off the road;
• promoting less polluting cars such as hybrid cars, electric cars and cars run on biofuels;
• congestion charges act as an extra tax on people bringing their cars into the city centre.

▼ **Rush hour in Los Angeles, USA. Ninety per cent of the people who work in Los Angeles travel into the city every day by car.**

'Restore human legs as a means of travel. Pedestrians rely on food for fuel and need no special parking facilities.'

Lewis Mumford (1895-1990), American writer and author of *The City in History* (1961)

Debate...
Congestion charges

Some cities, such as Singapore, Milan, Stockholm, Oslo and London, have implemented congestion charges: a compulsory daily fee for people driving into the city centre. There has been huge public opposition to congestion charges, but studies have shown that they are successful in reducing the number of cars in urban centres. They have also had a positive effect on air quality and have raised money for investment in public transport.

Should all city centres impose congestion charges? If not, why not?

'The experience of Bogotá shows that cities can prosper by focusing on a new model for success, one that is centered on the needs and contentment of all the city's residents – not just those that own a private car.'

Enrique Peñalosa, Mayor of Bogotá (1998-2001), speaking in 2003

Investing in public transport

Well-designed, energy-efficient public transport systems, such as trams, trains and buses, can encourage people to leave their cars at home and contribute to the sustainability of a city. But one solution cannot solve all transport problems. Bangkok (Thailand), Bogotá (Colombia), Amsterdam (the Netherlands) and Masdar (Abu Dhabi) are using a variety of transport solutions to improve their level of sustainability.

Case study...
Colombia: Bogotá

Bogotá (below) is a city of around 7 million people that decided to change its whole attitude to transportation in just three years (from 1998 to 2000). During this time:

• 250 km of bicycle tracks were created.
• The use of private cars was limited during the busiest traffic periods of the day.
• Hundreds of kilometres of pavements were laid to connect poor neighbourhoods with central parts of the city.
• A new rapid bus system, called TransMilenio, started running alongside the regular bus service in dedicated bus lanes.

The transport revolution that has taken place in Bogotá has happened alongside improvements in green space. Parks have been created and trees planted, so that the quality of life in Bogotá has greatly improved for its citizens.

Case study...
The Netherlands: Amsterdam

Germany, Denmark and China are all countries where a sizeable proportion of people use bicycles on a regular basis for commuting to and within cities, but Amsterdam is the only city in the world where recorded bike use outstrips car use. From 2005 to 2007, people living in Amsterdam got on their bicycles an average of 0.87 times a day – compared with making an average of 0.84 trips a day by car. People in Amsterdam now use their cars 14 per cent less than in 1990, and bicycle use has increased by 36 per cent. Amsterdam has a wide-ranging pattern of bicycle routes and the city's transport policy discriminates against cars. For example, it is difficult and expensive to find parking in the city centre, and cars in residential areas are not allowed to travel faster than 30 km an hour.

'People who normally drive, they know it will take five Euros for parking and take 10 minutes more than if they bike.'

Ralph Buehler, Professor of International Urban Affairs, Virginia Tech University, USA, talking about pro-bike policies in Amsterdam, 2009

▼ Amsterdam is one of the safest cities to be a cyclist in – only 1.1 Dutch cyclists are killed every 100 million km compared to 3.6 in the UK and 5.8 in the USA. It is thought that because more people are on bicycles, drivers are more aware of them on the road and so there are fewer accidents.

Case study...
Thailand:
Bangkok's rail
network

In Bangkok, an inefficient transport system and rapidly-increasing car ownership ensured that cars were the principal cause of poor air quality. In 1980, there were 600,000 cars on Bangkok's roads and this figure had increased to well over 5 million by 2007. In 2004, in an attempt to tackle Bangkok's traffic problems, the government invested in a new underground rail network and an above-ground monorail, called the Skytrain. Today, Bangkok is still a very polluted city, but the Skytrain construction programme is being expanded with the aim of improving air quality further.

▲ The Skytrain is the most comfortable way to travel around Bangkok – it is air-conditioned and fast, operating above the gridlocked and polluted streets of the Thai capital.

Case study...
Abu Dhabi:
Masdar

Masdar is a new eco-community for 50,000 people currently being built in Abu Dhabi's Arabian desert. Masdar has taken a radical approach to reducing car use – it has decided not to have any at all. Every inhabitant of Masdar will be within 200 metres of some form of public transport – either a light railway or a 'rapid transport pod'. These pods are small vehicles, currently used in the port of Rotterdam in the Netherlands to move containers around. They don't have drivers and run along tracks or magnetic discs set into the road surface. Masdar is committed to zero transport emissions.

▼ The model for Masdar, in Abu Dhabi.

Energy

All cities rely on burning fossil fuels, such as oil, gas, coal and wood, for their energy needs, and some rely on nuclear power as well. There are some cities that supplement fossil fuels with relatively small amounts of alternative energy, such as wind power, solar power, geothermal energy, hydroelectricity and energy generated from burning biomass (plant materials and animal waste). No city in the world has a large enough source of renewable energy to supply all of its energy via 'green' power, but this sector of the energy industry is growing all the time.

▼ **Basic small-scale solar panels installed on city roofs can heat the water that passes through them or more complex photovoltaic panels, such as the ones shown on this roof, can generate electricity by converting heat energy from the Sun into electricity that can be used in buildings.**

A carbon neutral future

When energy is produced from fossil fuels, carbon dioxide (CO_2) is released. CO_2 is thought to be a primary cause of man-made global warming. So to improve its sustainability, a city's carbon emissions need to be calculated and reduced. This can be done by improving energy-efficiency, reducing total energy consumption and obtaining energy from renewable sources. Carbon offsets – such as planting trees or putting money into the development of green technologies such as solar or wind power – can be purchased to bring down a city's carbon emissions further. A city that is not responsible for any overall carbon emissions is 'carbon neutral'.

'Though the emissions from the city of Sydney alone are small in terms of state, national and global emissions, we believe that our leadership can influence other governments by demonstrating that change is possible.'

Clover Moore, Lord Mayor of Sydney, 2009

Debate... Who should take the blame for CO_2?

Environmentalists disagree over where to place the blame for the majority of CO_2 emissions. Many scientists claim that cities are responsible for between 75 and 80 per cent of greenhouse gas emissions, and so the fight against climate change needs to be fought and won in cities.

But some environmentalists believe that cities are responsible for only 40 per cent of the greenhouse gases created by human activity, with agriculture (methane is produced by livestock, especially cows) and deforestation (CO_2 is released by burning trees), causing 30 per cent of emissions, and the remaining 30 per cent coming from industry, wealthy families, and power stations in the countryside powered by fossil fuels.

Why do you think that it is important to establish the correct facts in this debate?

Case study...

Australia: Sydney makes a start

There are currently no carbon-neutral cities in the world, but many city administrations and local governments are trying to find ways to reduce carbon emissions in city centres. In 2008, Sydney became Australia's first carbon-neutral local government. The part of the city that is carbon-neutral covers the central business district and some of the suburbs (around 26 sq km). Sydney examined the greenhouse gas emissions from a variety of sources, such as government-owned cars, streetlights, properties, business travel, contractors and suppliers. Energy efficiency strategies were then applied to all of these emissions sources, which included the government committing to buying 100 per cent of its energy from GreenPower (a renewable energy programme) and buying carbon offsets where needed.

▲ Sydney is part of the Climate Neutral Network, which was established by the United Nations Environment Programme (UNEP) to educate businesses, organisations, governments, and individuals about becoming carbon neutral.

A load of rubbish

The list of things we use and then throw away is very, very long – computers, DVD players, mobile phones, cars, carpets, food, cosmetics, garden waste, tyres, clothes, food, packaging, medications and plastic bags to name just some. Because cities contain huge populations of people, massive amounts of waste are produced and have to be collected, managed and disposed of safely. Cities have to reduce the amount of waste they create in order to reduce the environmental impact of that waste and to become more sustainable.

Wealthy cities

In well-established and wealthy cities, which are usually located in MDCs, people are charged local taxes that help pay for rubbish collection from right outside their homes. People in many MDCs sort and recycle their paper, plastics, glass and clothing and compost leftover food for use in gardens. There are public facilities where hazardous waste, such as paint, detergents, oil and batteries, can be deposited, and recycling collection points in supermarket car parks and other communal spaces. Waste that is not recycled is burned in incinerators that can produce harmful toxins or is buried in huge holes in the ground, called landfill sites. We will not always have enough landfill sites to cope with our rubbish so reducing, reusing and recycling really is important.

Zero waste cities

Zero waste means that, for example, individuals, businesses, organisations, villages, towns

▼ Wellington, New Zealand, aims to be a zero waste city by implementing initiatives, such as the Zero Waste campaign set up by the New Zealand Trust.

and cities should imitate nature by creating, using and recycling everything so that nothing has to be thrown away. With zero waste there isn't really any such thing as waste – because one person's waste can be used in a productive way by somebody else. Cities all over the world – such as San Francisco (USA), Wellington (New Zealand) and Canberra (Australia) – are working now to make changes that mean that they can become zero waste cities in the future.

Case study...
USA: San Francisco

San Francisco has an ambitious green objective – to become a zero waste city by 2020. San Francisco has banned plastic bags and styrofoam and enforces recycling at a local and government level. Recycling patrols check that homeowners are putting the right things into their recycling bins and restaurants that compost leftover food don't have to pay as much for rubbish collection. At the moment, an impressive 70 per cent of the waste that the city used to send to landfill sites is being diverted into composting, recycling and waste reduction. Composted material is sent to farms and vineyards outside the city, bringing recycling full circle.

'. . . we can break away from the medieval solutions of digging holes for our rubbish or setting it on fire. Burying or burning our household rubbish not only releases chemicals that are linked to horrific health problems but is a massive waste of energy and resources.'

Mark Strutt, Greenpeace campaigner, 2002

▼ San Francisco's 'Fantastic Three'. The city has three coloured recycling bins for different types of waste: blue (recyclables), black (non-recyclables and non-compostables), green (organic material).

Poor cities

Cities in less developed countries often don't have the money to put infrastructures in place to deal with the waste management and disposal problems created by their rapidly expanding populations. This can mean that uncollected domestic and industrial waste becomes a significant health hazard to the general population.

While these authorities may not have particularly effective waste management programmes, many of the poorest people in developing cities salvage everything they can of value from city waste dumps. This is highly dangerous work that only the most disadvantaged people in society undertake.

'Instead of accepting what our waste is and looking for ways to get rid of it, we should be asking why waste is produced and what it could become. As a source of pollution, rubbish needs to be controlled and hidden away. But treated as a resource it becomes a valuable material.'

Robin Murray, industrial economist, 2002

Case study...
Argentina: Buenos Aires' 'cardboard people'

It is thought that around 10,000 people in the city of Buenos Aires survive by collecting paper, cardboard and plastics which they sell to waste management companies for between 4p and 10p a kilo. These people are called *cartoneros* and many of them are women and children with little or no other means of earning a living. In 2008, the government of Buenos Aires decided to recognise the valuable job done by the *cartoneros* by formalising their role in the city's long-term recycling plan. The cartoneros are being encouraged to organise themselves into cooperatives with the promise that the government will then give them the task of collecting all the recyclable waste in the city for delivery to 'green centres' where they will be sorted for recycling. The work the *cartoneros* do reduces the amount of waste material being dumped in landfill sites and, because the *cartoneros* usually collect waste on foot, they are not contributing to emissions via petrol and diesel use.

◀ Recyclable waste in Buenos Aires is collected by individual people. Private waste management companies collect the remainder of the city's waste.

> 'Millions of tons of e-waste disappears from the developed world every year and continues to reappear in developing countries, despite international bans.'
>
> Luke Upchurch, Consumers International, 2008

▲ Scavenging old computers for re-saleable parts. Half a million old computers from more developed countries arrive in Lagos, Nigeria, every month.

Campaign... end e-waste exports

Greenpeace is campaigning to highlight the problems of exporting e-waste (dumped electronic goods) from MDCs to LDCs and to tighten up the policing of e-waste disposal in Europe. E-waste can leak harmful toxins and chemicals, so businesses and industries in the European Union countries are legally responsible for arranging for its safe disposal. Since 1992, there has been a European ban (called the Basel Ban) on exporting e-waste to LDCs, but despite this, millions of computers arrive in countries such as Ghana and Nigeria every year. Children scour the mountains of computers in city dumps in Lagos and break into the machines in search of metals to sell. In Accra, the capital of Ghana, kids burn the insides of the computers to get at metals such as copper, unaware of the toxic fumes they are breathing in.

How much waste?

• New York City produces 36,200 tons of waste every day.
• 12,500 tons of waste are produced every day in Mexico City.
• The European Environment Agency (EEA) anticipates an increase in city waste in the European Union between 2005 and 2020 of 25 per cent.

Water

Cities consume huge amounts of water – individual households use water for drinking, gardening, waste disposal, cooking and washing, and businesses and industry use water in even greater quantities. Cities can either be great places to access water – millions of people get clean, constant water at the turn of a tap – or dreadful places where drinking water is drawn directly from sewers, comes in expensive bottled form, or is unregulated and unreliable.

▼ School children in Jakarta, Indonesia, learning how to wash clothes. Less than 25 per cent of the people in Jakarta have access to clean, piped water.

'The challenge will have to be met in the coming decades. In our cities and megacities, where most people will live, much water will be consumed and most of the pollution will be generated.'

Kalyan Ray, Water for African Cities Programme, 2002

Conserving water

Cities take water resources from the areas that surround them – sometimes there is not enough water to go around and they pump water in from hundreds of kilometres away. Water conservation is essential if cities are to become more sustainable.

Supplying water

Water infrastructures – thousands of kilometres of pipes, purification facilities, and sewers supplied by safe and plentiful water sources – are complex and expensive and require continuous monitoring. Developed cities with steady and predictable populations are wealthy enough to build and update these kinds of water systems, but developing cities with rising populations grow too quickly and haphazardly to put water supply networks in place. People in developing cities have restricted access to water and sanitation – if they have any at all – and this impacts on their health due to the rapid spread of water-borne diseases.

Restoring the water cycle

In many cities there is enough water to go around because the water that falls as rain on to the city should replenish the watershed that the city sits in. But very often rivers have been concreted over and canals and drainage systems created in their place. This means that rain doesn't find its way back into the groundwater store, but hits concrete and runs off into drains or is channelled via pipelines away from the city to prevent flooding. Some cities, such as Los Angeles, are working to get rid of the concrete, plant trees and capture and store rainwater so that a more natural water cycle can be restored and the city can retain more of the water that falls within its watershed.

▼ Los Angeles is always short of water – it has to import 50 per cent of what it needs – but a lot of the city's water is wasted because rainfall is collected in storm drains (left of picture) that then empty into the sea.

'With the population of cities expected to increase to five billion by 2025, the urban demand for water is set to increase exponentially. This means that any solution to the water crisis is closely linked to the governance of cities.'

Klaus Toepfer, Executive Director of the United Nations Environment Programme (UNEP), 2005

Campaign...
Water for African Cities Programme

The Water for African Cities Programme is supported by the UN-HABITAT programme. One of the UN's Millennium Development Goals is to reduce by 50 per cent the number of people in the world who do not have access to sanitation and clean water by 2015. The Water for African Cities Programme has been set up to try to achieve this by managing water more efficiently, protecting freshwater resources, promoting conservation and spreading education about water issues to people living in urban areas.

Megacities

egacities are cities with a population of 10 million or more. In 1970, there were only three megacities – New York (USA), Shanghai (China) and Tokyo (Japan) – but by 2000 there were 19. By 2020, the world could be home to anything between 23 and 33 megacities.

▶ **New York City in the evening. This megacity has an estimated population of over 21 million people. The USA also has another megacity – Los Angeles – with a population of around 18 million people.**

'A greater concentration of populations in urban centres is expected to help governments develop policies aimed at sustainable use of natural resources.'

Hania Zlotnik, Director of the United Nations Department of Economic and Social Affairs' Population Division, 2008

Megacity facts

• The biggest city in the world today is Tokyo, with a population of over 35 million including the greater Tokyo area.
• Lagos, Nigeria, is the fastest-growing city in the world – 58 people are added to its population every hour.
• Other fast-growing cities include Kinshasa (Democratic Republic of Congo), Lahore and Karachi (both in Pakistan) and Dhaka (Bangladesh).

The balance shifts

There has been a shift in the geography of megacities. Megacities first appeared in countries with large economies, but now 14 out of the 19 megacities in the world are in developing nations and it is predicted that of the 23 megacities of 2020, only four of them will be in the developed world.

Why megacities are important

Cities in the developing world are growing so rapidly that there often is not enough time or money to create adequate infrastructures in areas such as housing, power generation, sewage disposal, clean water monitoring and transport. Without environmentally-sensitive investment and planning, megacities are unsustainable and unstoppable.

'The tearing down of the motorway has had both intended and unexpected effects. As soon as we destroyed the road, the cars just disappeared and drivers changed their habits. A lot of people just gave up their cars.'

Kee Yeon Hwang, Professor of Urban Planning, Hongik University, South Korea, talking about the effects of restoring the Cheonggyecheon river, 2006

The Cheonggyecheon area in Seoul is now home to a thriving ecosystem, a new museum, running tracks, and walkways.

Case study...
South Korea: Seoul – changing megacities

Seoul is a megacity of just over 10 million people and, until recently, the city was cut in half by a six-lane motorway built over the top of the concreted-over bed of the Cheonggyecheon river. Over 160,000 cars used the motorway every day. In 2002 the Mayor of Seoul, Lee Myung Bak, promised to demolish the motorway, put back the river and create a park in the middle of the city. From 2003-05 the motorway was dismantled and taken away, the river restored, new bus services into the city added, and alternative roads and bridges built. People now flock to the river for recreation all year round, use their cars less and report an increase in the quality of life. Air quality has improved, wildlife and plants have returned, 50 per cent more wind rushes through the city to cool it and the river has lowered the temperature of the area around it by an average of 3.6 degrees in the summer.

Cities of the future

The future of cities is big – there will be more and more cities and they will get larger and larger. The question is 'Will these cities be sustainable?'

Changing cities

At the moment cities are not sustainable, but numerous cities in developed nations around the world are improving their sustainability in response to economic, political and social pressures. As economies advance in developing nations, improvements are taking place as people become better educated and demand higher standards of basic things like cleaner air and water.

◀ The French president hopes that green spaces, like this park in Paris, will be part of the Greater Paris expansion.

'Greater Paris is about the capital playing a role in the European and the world economy [and becoming] a sustainable city for the post-Kyoto era.'

Nicolas Sarkozy, President of France, 29 April, 2009

Is the future of cities already here?

The answer to this question is possibly. Properly managed cities can become the key to future sustainability. Massive concentrations of people living on relatively small areas of land can make a positive contribution to preserving natural resources, as long as investments are made in things such as renewable energy, urban farms and public transport systems.

'These eco-towns will not only provide for local communities, they will be a showcase of what is possible nationally and also internationally.'

Caroline Flint, UK housing minister, 2008

▼ Eco-towns, such as BedZED in the UK, are powerful political statements, but are they environmentally sound?

Debate...
UK: Eco-towns – good or bad?

The British government wants to build up to ten new eco-towns over the next decade.

For eco-towns
• Environmental building needs to improve and sustainable urban developments need to demonstrate how they can work. Eco-towns will help to set new standards in these areas.
• Eco-towns will provide affordable housing to many and will help the country achieve its targets for emissions reductions.

Against eco-towns
• It takes an average of 50 years to recoup the extra expense of green building and the construction of new housing is totally unsustainable – all buildings should be conserved and retrofitted with green features, such as extra insulation, before any new homes are built.
• Regardless of how green the finished buildings will be, eco-towns still involve construction that uses up natural resources, destroys the countryside, and disrupts wildlife.

Do you think we should build eco-towns or not? Would it be better to invest in higher-density housing in existing cities and retrofitting old buildings?

Glossary

Alternative energy: any form of energy that can be captured from renewable sources, such as wind, tidal or solar power. They are alternatives to non-renewable energy sources.

Biodiversity: the variety of plant and animal species that live in an area.

BREEAM: stands for the BRE Environmental Assessment Method. This is a British environmental building standard but it is also used all over the world. BREEAM includes a Code for Sustainable Homes.

Brownfield: a site within a city that has been previously developed but has fallen into disrepair or is no longer used.

Carbon dioxide (CO_2): a gas found in the atmosphere that is used by plants during photosynthesis, but is also believed to contribute to man-made global warming.

Carbon neutral: having no net carbon emissions.

Carbon offsets: a technology or scheme that seeks to reduce carbon dioxide and help individuals or businesses become carbon neutral by balancing emissions with actions or activities which reduce emissions.

E-waste: old, unwanted electronic goods.

Earth Summit: the popular name given to the United Nations Conference on Environmental and Development that was held in Rio de Janeiro, Brazil, in 1992.

Ecological footprint: the amount of natural resources used by an individual or place.

Food miles: the distance food is transported before it reaches the table of the person eating it.

Greenbelt: protected green space surrounding a city.

Green Star: began in 2003 in Australia and is a voluntary green building rating scheme. Buildings are rated according to their sustainability and energy efficiency.

Infant mortality: the number of children who die before the age of one. Infant mortality is measured for every 1,000 live births.

Landfill: a hole in the ground used to dump waste materials.

LEED: stands for Leadership in Energy and Environmental Design and is the USA's environmental building standard award scheme.

Peri-urban: is the name given to land next to an urban area, between the suburbs and open countryside.

Suburbs: are the areas surrounding cities that are predominately residential.

Urban cultivation: the production of food on land given over to farming within cities.

Urban planning: planning all the elements of a city, such as transport, green space, waste disposal, recycling, housing, leisure and office space, so that they all work efficiently and beneficially for the inhabitants.

Urban sprawl: the uncontrolled spread of cities beyond the suburbs into rural areas. Urban sprawl puts a further strain on natural resources and impacts on wildlife and plants.

Watershed: the area of land which drains into a specific river and its tributaries.

Zero waste: this term was devised by Robin Murray, a British industrial economist who came up with the idea that a use should be found for as much waste as possible rather than just dumping it in landfill sites or burning it.

Websites

Dharavi slum website
www.dharavi.org
A website about Dharavi slum where slum dwellers have posted photographs of their communities and businesses, stories and information.

Greenpeace
www.greenpeace.org.uk
Greenpeace website with pages on e-waste and digital dumping. Go to 'Poisoning the poor – electronic waste in Ghana' to watch a 6-minute film on the effects of electronic waste in Ghana.

Greening of Detroit
www.greeningofdetroit.com
The website of the Greening of Detroit campaign. Interesting links to past and current projects, photo gallery and educational resources.

Global Footprint Network
www.footprintnetwork.org
A website dedicated to advancing the science of sustainability.

Sustainable Cities
www.sustainablecities.org.uk
An organisation that brings together business and cities to rethink the way urban areas are designed and used.

Christian Aid
www.christianaid.org.uk
Find out more about Christian Aid's work to expose and battle the scandal of poverty.

Urban Age
www.urban-age.net
A website about the future of cities with contributions from world-famous architects and urban planners.

Water for African Cities Programme
www.unhabitat.org
The website of the UN-supported campaign to improve water supply to urban areas of Africa.

YouTube: Bogotá, building a sustainable city
www.youtube.com/watch?v=EuaXcRtgPzE
A podcast by the former Mayor of Bogotá about the challenges involved in creating a sustainable city.

Campaign for Better Transport
www.bettertransport.org.uk
The website of the UK's leading transport campaign group includes activities, campaigns, and information on how to get involved.

San Francisco Planning Department
www.sfgov.org/site/planning_index. asp?id=25288
A website including reports, maps and more information about the San Francisco Eastern Neighborhoods Programme.

Please note: every effort has been made by the Publishers to ensure that these websites contain no inappropriate or offensive material. However, because of the nature of the Internet, it is impossible to guarantee that the contents of these sites will not be altered. We strongly advise that Internet access is supervised by a responsible adult.

Index